百年南开正青春

Youthful

NKU

and Its 100 Years

南开大学出版社
天 津

图书在版编目(CIP)数据

百年南开正青春 / 吴军辉编. —天津：南开大学
出版社，2019.8
　(南开永远年青丛书)
　ISBN 978-7-310-05878-5

　Ⅰ.①百… Ⅱ.①吴… Ⅲ.①南开大学－概况－图集
Ⅳ.①G649.282.1－64

中国版本图书馆 CIP 数据核字(2019)第 181265 号

南开大学出版社出版发行
出版人：刘运峰
地址：天津市南开区卫津路 94 号　　邮政编码：300071
营销部电话：(022)23508339　23500755
营销部传真：(022)23508542　　邮购部电话：(022)23502200

*

北京隆晖伟业彩色印刷有限公司印刷
全国各地新华书店经销

*

2019 年 8 月第 1 版　　2019 年 8 月第 1 次印刷
285×210 毫米　16 开本　13.5 印张　4 插页　200 千字
定价：108.00 元

如遇图书印装质量问题，请与本社营销部联系调换，电话：(022)23507125

总　序

扎根于中国大地的南开大学，走过了不平凡的一百年。

百年风雨，百年坎坷；百年激昂，百年奋进。南开大学的发展始终与国家民族命运紧相连，与时代社会的发展相偕行。百年的足迹承载着中国大学的初心与梦想，记录了中国大学的苦难与荣光，见证了中国大学的成熟和积淀。这征程，一走就是一百年。弦歌不辍，步履不停。

一百年来，无数南开人为民族谋独立，为中华谋复兴，为人类求新知。以无数南开人的志向，成就南开大学的志向；以无数南开人的奋斗，发出南开大学的光芒；以无数南开人的青春，织就南开大学的青春。青春不朽，歌声不散。

百年校庆，是里程碑，是宣言书，是纪念册，是新起点。为了献礼百年校庆，我们策划出版了"南开永远年青"丛书，铭记艰险的征途，缅怀前行的勇者，传唱青春的诗篇。丛书包括《百年南开正青春》（图册）、《一百个南开故事》、《湖畔行吟——〈南开大学报〉"新开湖"副刊百期选粹》，记录了南开百年里的青春瞬间，书写了山水相逢的青春故事，描绘了校园生活的多姿多彩，展现南开人的月异日新。

1931 年 11 月 9 日，正是中华民族忧患深重的时候，张伯苓老校长让学生记住："国家是我们的，领土是我们的，时间也是我们的，努力！前进！奋斗！"当前，中华民族正走在复兴大道上，南开大学也将迈上新征程。以青春之心努力、前进、奋斗，我们不会老去，南开永远年青！

是为序。

马长虹

2019 年 8 月 28 日

渤海之滨，白河之津，巍巍南开精神。陶铸英才，传承文明，泱泱学府北辰。

百年南开栉风沐雨、披荆斩棘，一路高歌猛进。她，于峥嵘岁月中守正传承，于时代盛世下开拓创新。回望历史，这是一个世纪艰难创业的积淀，更是新世纪破浪航行的发端。百年，之于历史长河，短短一瞬；之于南开，恰风华正茂！当青春遇上南开，它便拥有了更多含义，它是魅力，是勇气，是自信，是拼搏，是海纳百川、融汇中西，更是追求卓越、孤勇锐意。

大学之魂，在学人风骨；大学之美，在校园风物。看今朝南开，智勇真纯的莘莘学子、妙语传芳的白发先生、筑梦四海的万千校友，连同襟怀宏阔的主楼、饱经沧桑的校钟、书香四溢的图书馆、树影斑驳的大中路、菡萏飘香的马蹄湖、激扬汗水的运动场，一草一木，碑刻雕塑，无不述说着南开人奋斗的青春。

青春，是这座百年学府惯有的气质，更是深得"允公允能，日新月异"校训浸润之南开人的可贵面貌。时光代序、岁月轮回，青春之南开永葆生机活力；十秩峥嵘、薪火相传，今日之南开必将续写新百年的辉煌！

By the Bohai Sea and the Peiho River,Roots the sublime spirit of Nankai.Where intellects are nurtured, culture inherited,Shines the grand North Star of Education.

In the past century, Nankai University (NKU) has made great strides through a thorny road, achieving epic progress along the way. In the years of tortuousness, she managed to uphold her integrity and sustain her spirit. In times of prosperity, she has been a pioneer to blaze new trails. For her, the past century has been an arduous journey of accumulation and endeavors, but it is also the beginning of a brave and ambitious voyage in the new century. For the long course of history, a century just takes place in the blink of an eye; but for NKU, it heralds the bloom of her youth! At NKU, youth is endowed with multiple meanings. It means charm, courage, confidence, and persistence, means openness to diversity and integration of Chinese and western cultural essence, as well as the pursuit of excellence and the audacity to fight alone with perseverance.

The soul of a university lies in the spirit of its scholars and students, and the beauty of a university exists in its buildings and landscapes. At today's NKU, you can see bright students with brave and pure hearts, hoary-headed professors with wit and wisdom, and numerous alumni fulfilling their aspirations all over the world. You can also see the majestic main building, the weathered school bell, and the book-laden library, as well as the Dazhong Road with latticed shadows of leaves, the Mati Lake with the fragrance of lotus, and the sports ground with the sweat shed by students. Everything on campus, either grasses and trees or inscriptions and sculptures, all tells about the youth of the strivers at NKU.

Youth is an intrinsic nature of this century-old university. It is also a valuable feature of people at NKU, who are deeply influenced by NKU's motto of "Dedication to public interests, acquisition of all-round capability, and aspiration for progress with each passing day". No matter how time flies and seasons shift, youth and vitality still blossom here at NKU. With ten extraordinary decades and continuous inheritance, today's NKU will move on to create a new century of glory!

目录
CONTENTS

第一章

忆芳华

Reminiscences of the Blooming Years

守护老图的铜狮子
高 鹏 摄
The copper lion guarding the Old Library
Photo by Gao Peng

第一章　忆芳华

Chapter I　Reminiscences of the Blooming Years

她，肇端于民族危亡，诞生于五四风雷，不惧日军炮火，千里跋涉，于祖国西南为民族存续文明火种……百年南开，始终与国家民族命运紧相联，与时代社会发展相偕行，它承载着"一群不服输的中国人"的初心与梦想，见证了中国高等教育筚路蓝缕的奋斗与荣光！

菁菁校园，诉说百年芳华。万千南开学子最爱主楼的恢宏大气；总理像前，轻道一声"我也是爱南开的"，说不尽浓情厚意；途经凝重古朴的校钟、巍然仁立的联大碑，张伯苓老校长的"爱国三问"，如洪钟大吕，警醒神州；漫步于思源堂、秀山堂、木斋馆之间，品一品历经风雨而愈难愈开的百年传奇……光影之间，迦陵学舍、陈省身故居、伯苓楼、范孙楼、东艺楼，留下了代代南开人的青春印记。寻一本书，躲进老图的宁静里，感受百年学府的青春气息！

NKU was established in 1919, when the thunder of the May Fourth Movement was just about to explode and the whole China just fell into a life-and-death crisis. For the survival of the nation's civilization, NKU trekked across the country for thousands of miles to the southwestern corner, fearless of Japanese gun fires. During the past century, NKU has always been closely linked with the fate of the nation, advancing together with the progress of the society. Bearing the original aspiration and pursuit of a group of Chinese who never surrender, it has witnessed the arduous endeavors and inspiring glories of China's higher education.

The vigorous campus itself is a narrator of NKU's eventful years in the past century. A myriad of NKU students admire the main building for its grandeur and magnificence. In front of the statue of Premier Zhou Enlai, they can't express their deep affection for NKU, murmuring "I love NKU, too!" to the statue. When stopping by the solemn and aged school bell and the towering monument of the National Southwest Associated University, they can hear the Three Questions for Patriotism asked by the founding president Zhang Boling, which resonated across China and awakened the whole nation. Walking between the Siyuan Hall, the Xiushan Hall, and the Muzhai Library, they can experience a century's legend of going through storms and overcoming hardships. In other buildings, such as the Jialing Academy, the Former Residence of Chern Shiing-shen, the Boling Building, the Fansun Building, and the Building of Eastern Arts, they can see the traces of Nankai people's youth preserved in each passing moment. They can find a book, hide in the tranquility of the old library, and feel the youth of this century-old university.

昔日城南开洼地 今日城市正中心
杨宝诚 · 摄
The then wash land in the city's south has become today's city center
Photo by Yang Yucheng

南开创办人严修塑像
吴军辉 摄
Statue of Yan Fansun (Yan Xiu), the founder of Nankai University
Photo by Wu Junhui

南开创办人张伯苓塑像

吴军辉 摄

Statue of Zhang Boling, the founding president of Nankai University

Photo by Wu Junhui

主楼巍巍塑英华
常小松 摄
The magnificent main building in which illustrious talent are taught
Photo by Chang Xiaosong

雪夜里的西南联大纪念碑
刘瑞麒 摄
Monument of the National Southwest Associated University on a snowy night
Photo by Liu Ruiqi

思源堂
常小松 摄
Siyuan Hall of Nankai university
Photo by Chang Xiaosong

东校门
林坤洋 摄

East gate of Nankai University
Photo by Lin Kunyang

陈省身数学研究所
聂际慈 摄
Chern Institute of Mathematics
Photo by Nie Jici

春雨
高 鹏 摄
Spring rain

新开湖畔 "读书少女" 塑像

吴军辉 摄

The statue of "A Reading Girl" by the Xinkai Lake

Photo by Wu Junhui

杨石先塑像
常小松 摄
Statue of Yang Shixian
Photo by Chang Xiaosong

第六教学楼（昆虫学研究所）
王烁皓 摄
The Sixth Teaching Building (Institute of Entomology)
Photo by Wang Shuohao

碧波如洗的新开湖
林坤洋 摄

The clear Xinkai Lake in blue waves
Photo by Lin Kunyang

范孙楼
王烁皓 摄
Fansun Building
Photo by Wang Shuohao

风雪中的西南联大建校 50 周年纪念碑
吴军辉 摄

Monument to the 50th Anniversary of the National Southwest
Associated University in Snow
Photo by Wu Junhui

银装素裹的校园
吴军辉 摄

Campus in silver white snow
Photo by Wu Junhui

静谧的大中路
高　鹏　摄

The tranquil Dazhong Road
Photo by Gao Peng

雪夜里的周恩来纪念碑
刘瑞麒 摄

Monument of Zhou Enlai on a snowy night
Photo by Liu Ruiqi

迦陵学舍
王晓明 摄
Jialing Academy
Photo by Wang Xiaoming

马蹄湖畔老教材中心礼堂一角
王晓明 摄

A corner at the Auditorium of the Old Textbook
Center by Mati Lake
Photo by Wang Xiaoming

生命科学学院
王烁皓 摄
College of Life Sciences
Photo by Wang Shuohao

化学楼
王烁皓 摄
Chemistry Building
Photo by Wang Shuohao

经济学院大楼
姜丙骏 摄
Building of the College of Economics
Photo by Jiang Bingjun

泰达学院
王烁皓 摄
TEDA College
Photo by Wang Shuohao

身边的校徽
吴军辉 摄
University emblem around us
Photo by Wu Junhui

学校办公楼
天南大联合研究院

亭亭净植不蔓不枝
吴军辉　摄
Standing straight neither spreading about nor branching out
Photo by Wu Junhui

第二章

香满径

Roads Full of Fragrance

彩虹
王晓明 摄
Rainbow
Photo by Wang Xiaoming

第二章 香满径

Chapter II Roads Full of Fragrance

携百年风韵，古朴而端庄大气；融现代之美，出新而惹人叹奇。四季皆令人沉醉，这便是南开之美。春风细雨、夏意葱茏、秋高气爽、冬雪纷飞、海棠醒了又眠、梨园散了又聚、荷花开了又谢、雪花落了又起，四季分明的南开园，变幻出无穷的美丽。

这里是知识的殿堂，是创新的高地，但并不妨碍她拥抱诗情画意和花香鸟语。一花一草皆生命，一枝一叶总关情。当苦读之余，瞥见三教窗外的一树桃花或是七教墙上的大片枫藤；当好友交谈，踏着新开湖畔的落叶金黄或是伴着西区路旁的蔷薇飘香；当偶遇烦恼，散心于笔直坦阔的大中路，听着风吹白杨窸窣作响；当携手爱情，走遍校园每个角落，赏遍四时风光……那一瞬间，南开的脉脉温情便在学子的心底深深镌刻。念旧日时光，记青春畅想，钟灵毓秀，满径花香，代代学子饱览南开之美，一花一木涵养了人文气质，留下了一个又一个关于青春的故事。

The long years in the past century has brought vintage, simple and magnificent graces to the campus of NKU, while contemporary aesthetics has embedded it with novel and stunning beauty. NKU, with its own charm, is fascinating in different seasons. Here at NKU, seasons have their distinctive features, creating changeable and infinite beauty with the drizzling spring rain, the flourishing summer green, the refreshing autumn air, the flying winter snow, and the adorable flowers that blossom and fade away in turn.

NKU is the solemn palace of knowledge and the rigorous hub of innovation, but this does not prevent her from embracing a poetic life to appreciate fragrant flowers and singing birds. Either grasses and flowers or branches and leaves, they are all soulful living beings. There are moments when NKU engraves its tenderness deep within students' hearts. Such moments take place when students look up from their books, catching a glimpse of a peach blossom outside the window of the Third Teaching Building or a vast patch of ivy on the wall of the Seventh Teaching Building; when students chat with their friends, stepping on the golden fallen leaves by the Xinkai Lake or smelling the fragrance of the roses along the westside roads; when students disturbed by troubles take a walk along the straight and broad Dazhong Road, listening to the window blowing the poplar leaves; when students walk over the campus with their beloved ones, appreciating the views in different seasons… Generations of students have enjoyed the beauty of NKU, walking along the roads full of fragrant flowers, recalling the old days, and remembering the wild dreams in youth. The flowers and trees have cultivated NKU's humanistic qualities and endowed it with natural elegance, recording stories about the youth.

最是春日好读书
王俊峰 摄
Spring is the prime time for reading
Photo by Wang Junfeng

敬业广场一侧花树下嬉戏的小朋友
游思行 摄

Children playing under the flowering trees on the side
of the Jingye Square
Photo by You Sihang

花香与晚读相伴
林坤洋 摄

Fragrance of flowers accompanies evening reading
Photo by Lin Kunyang

物理学院楼西侧的桃花
吴军辉 摄
Peach blossoms on the west side of the School of
Physics Building
Photo by Wu Junhui

梨园飘香新校园
史　嵩摄

Pear Garden in new blossoms that covers
the campus with fragrance
Photo by Shi Song

梨花掩映图书馆
刘瑞麒 摄
Library hidden in pear blossoms
Photo by Liu Ruiqi

春日的油菜花田
刘瑞麟 摄
Rapeseed field in spring
Photo by Liu Ruiqi

敬业广场的海棠花海
刘瑞麟 摄

The sea of begonia flower at the Jingye Square
Photo by Liu Ruiqi

那年夏天的大中路
吴军辉 摄

Dazhong Road in that summer
Photo by Wu Junhui

仲夏夜的新开湖
王晓明 摄

Xinkai Lake in a midsummer night
Photo by Wang Xiaoming

一池清夏
韦承金 摄

A pool of summer
Photo by Wei Chengjin

西区公寓绽放的蔷薇
高 鹏 摄

Blooming Roses at West Area Apartment
Photo by Gao Peng

津南校区东北角湿地的黑翅长脚鹬
姜丙骏 摄

Himantopus in the northeast tip wetland at Jinnan Campus
Photo by Jiang Bingjun

津南校区马蹄湖中的黑天鹅
姜丙骏 摄

Black Swan in the Mati Lake at Jinnan Campus
Photo by Jiang Bingjun

南开秋韵
王晓明 摄
Nankai University with a taste of autumn
Photo by Wang Xiaoming

路过秋天
王晓明 摄
Passing autumn
Photo by Wang Xiaoming

第二章 · 香满径 51
Chapter II · Roads Full of Fragrance

有缘落在南开园的雪花
王晓明　摄

Snowflakes that fall in the Nankai Garden
Photo by Wang Xiaoming

雪中英桐
王晓明　摄

The London plane tree in snow
Photo by Wang Xiaoming

雪中"海棠花"（大通学生中心）
王海琦 摄
"Begonia flower" in snow(Datong student center)
Photo by Wang Haiqi

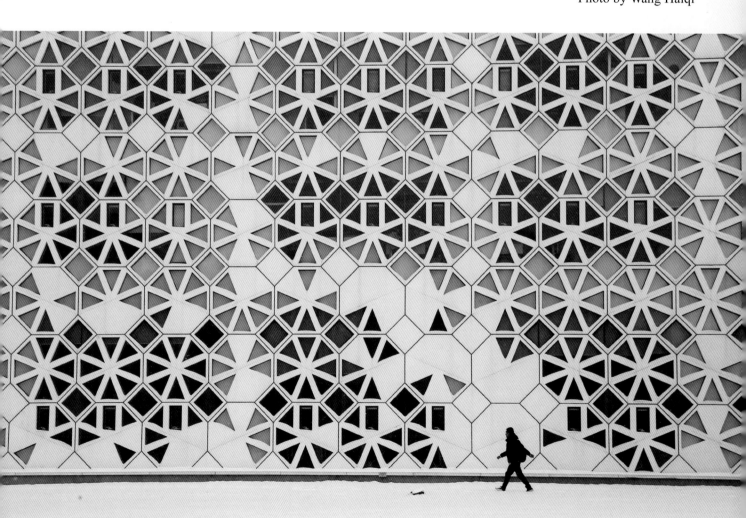

冬季冰凌美景
王晓明 摄

Beautiful scene of ice in winter
Photo by Wang Xiaoming

南开雪夜
刘瑞麒 摄
Nankai University on a snowy night
Photo by Liu Ruiqi

大中路雪景
刘瑞麒 摄
Dazhong Road in snow
Photo by Liu Ruiqi

"九·一八"纪念活动
王晓明 摄
"9·18" commemoration events
Photo by Wang Xiaoming

第二章

育人杰

Cultivation of Outstanding Talent

舞蹈社团学生在新校区学生活动中心"海棠花"排练
王晓明 摄

Dance club students are rehearsing at the "Begonia
Flower" student center at the new campus
Photo by Wang Xiaoming

第三章 育人杰
Chapter III Cultivation of Outstanding Talent

百年薪火，桃李芬芳，这里走出了共和国开国总理周恩来、我国农药化学和元素有机化学奠基人杨石先、数学大师陈省身、物理学家吴大猷、戏剧家曹禺、"两弹一星"功勋科学家郭永怀、地质学家刘东生……他们都有着共同的名字——"南开人"。

他们都是在青春的年纪，走进这方校园，带着对知识的渴望，对未来的憧憬，带着改造世界的无尽热情，负笈苦读，汲取滋养，努力拼搏，立公增能。荣耀百年育人杰，青春南开再出发。这里有德业双馨的良师益友，有精深广博的专业课程，有爱国报国的浓厚氛围，有丰富多彩的校园文化，有文体并重的社团活动，有崇尚劳动的价值追求，有锐意创新的精神沃土。这是一座伟大的学府，历经百年文脉不曾断过一刻；这是一座伟大的学校，"育才为国"初心代代传承。多彩的梦想、一样的飞翔。当青春遇上南开，定会绽放更加璀璨的光芒。

With a century's inheritance, NKU has cultivated a remarkable number of highly reputed students. PRC's first premier Zhou Enlai, the founder of China's pesticide chemistry and elemental organic chemistry Yang Shixian, mathematician Chern Shiing-shen, physicist Wu Ta-you, playwright Cao Yu, one of the main contributors to the Two Bombs and One Satellite Project Guo Yonghuai, and geologist Liu Dongsheng… they all start here from NKU.

They entered NKU at young ages, with desires for knowledge, aspirations for the future, and endless enthusiasm to reshape the world. Making studious efforts to absorb new knowledge, they strived to enhance their abilities for their commitment to public well-being. With a century's glorious endeavors to cultivate talents, the youthful NKU has set out to start again. At NKU, there are virtuous and outstanding mentors, in-depth and extensive professional courses, various arts and sports activities, as well as a strong and patriotic atmosphere, a rich and diversified campus culture, a steadfast value of advocating labor works, and a profound belief in innovation. It is a great university, which has never stopped its cultural continuity in the past century. It is a great education institution, which has inherited the mission of cultivating intellects for the nation from generation to generation. Students might have different dreams to chase, but NKU makes sure that they can all get their wings to fly up high. The youth of NKU will bloom and shine more brightly.

薪火相传：南开大学 4 岁小朋友看望 104 岁经济学家杨敬年
姜宝成 摄

Passing the flame: 4-year-old children visiting the 104-year-old economist
Yang Jingnian at Nankai University
Photo by Jiang Baocheng

著名化学家、中国科学院院士申泮文与学生一起参加长跑活动
游思行 摄

Shen Panwen, a famous chemist and academician of Chinese Academy of
Sciences, participating in the long-distance running with students
Photo by You Sihang

叶嘉莹先生
聂际慈 摄

Ye Jiaying Xiansheng (a honorific title to show respect
to someone who has achieved a certain level of mastery)
Photo by Nie Jici

中国工程院院士李正名与学生交流
聂际慈 摄

Li Zhengming, an academician of Chinese Academy of Engineering, communicating with students
Photo by Nie Jici

中国科学院院士葛墨林给学生授课

韦承金 摄

Ge Molin, an ademician of Chinese Academy of
Sciences, is teaching students

Photo by Wei Chengjin

南开大学终身教授范曾举办讲座
刘东岳 摄

Fan Zeng, a tenured professor of Nankai University, giving a
lecture to teachers and students
Photo by Liu Dongyue

2017 年南开大学 8 名参军入伍大学生行前合影
（左起：胡一帆、蔚晨阳、阿斯哈尔·努尔太、王晗、贾岚珺、戴蕊、李业广、董旭东）
新闻中心资料图
a group of 8 students from Nankai University taking a photo before leaving to enlist in the
army in 2017 (from the left: Hu Yifan, Yu Chenyang, Ashar Nurtai, Wang Han, Jia Lanjun,
Dai Rui, Li Yeguang, Dong Xudong)
Photo /NKU News Center

入伍八学子之一阿斯哈尔·努尔太正在进行征兵宣传
王晓明 摄

Ashar Nurtai, one of the eight enlisted students, publicizing conscription
Photo by Wang Xiaoming

立志报国　新兵送行
刘东岳　摄
Determined to serve the country,seeing off new recruits
Photo by Liu Dongyue

一名学生在展示参军光荣纪念章
王晓明 摄

A student showing the enlisting honor medal
Photo by Wang Xiaoming

校钟长鸣　勿忘国耻

任永华　摄

School bell tolling to remember the national shame
Photo by Ren Yonghua

联大碑前缅怀先烈
姜宝成 摄

Commemorating martyrs in front of the Monument of National Southwest Associated University
Photo by Jiang Baocheng

纪念于方舟烈士
李　想摄
Commemorating Martyr Yu Fangzhou
Photo by Li Xiang

学生擦拭墓碑缅怀数学大师陈省身
姜宝成 摄

Students wiping the tombstones to remember the
mathematics master Chern Shiing-shen
Photo by Jiang Baocheng

法国高等科学研究所（IHES）在南开大学
举办著名数学家图片展纪念陈省身先生
李　想摄

The French Institute of Advanced Science (IHES) holding a photo
exhibition of famous mathematicians at Nankai University to commemorate
Mr. Chern Shiing-shen
Photo by Li Xiang

学生奋力拼搏，打破校运会跳高记录

任永华 摄

Students tried hard and broke the high jump record in
the university sports games
Photo by Ren Yonghua

"活力南开"群体性活动学生跆拳道展演
王晓明 摄
Taekwondo show, one of the "Vibrant Nankai" student
group activities
Photo by Wang Xiaoming

正在训练的南开大学龙舟队

张珀瑜 摄

The Nankai University Dragon Boat Team in training

Photo by Zhang Poyu

2017 届毕业生展示体质健康证书等
李晓彤 摄

A 2017 graduate showing her physique health certificate and so on
Photo by Li Xiaotong

同学们举行地球熄灯一小时活动
王晓明 摄

Students observing the Earth Hour lights off activity
Photo by Wang Xiaoming

深夜的图书馆，同学们依旧沉浸学习之中
林坤洋 摄
Students still immersed in learning at the library late at night
Photo by Lin Kunyang

开学第一天，一名学生在津南新校区图书馆读书
吴军辉 摄
A student reading at the Jinnan New Campus Library on the
first day of school
Photo by Wu Junhui

京剧名家马少良为大学生们讲授
"京剧与戏曲文化"，并演示京剧四功五法
姜宝成 摄

Ma Shaoliang, the famous Beijing opera master, teaching "Beijing
Opera and Opera Culture" to students, and demonstrating Beijing
Opera's four exercises and five methods
Photo by Jiang Baocheng

中学生走进南开大学实验室利用电子显微镜了解纳米材料的秘密
王晓明 摄

Middle school students visiting Nankai University laboratory to understand the
secrets of nanomaterials using electron microscopy
Photo by Wang Xiaoming

科技周活动中南开老师为孩子们讲解植物分类
沈 岳 摄

Teachers from Nankai University explaining plant classification
to the children in the Science and Technology Week
Photo by Shen Yue

南开大学"农梦成真"创业团队负责人彭俊
在山西与枣农一同挑选红枣，通过电商助农增收
聂际慈 摄

Peng Jun, the leader of the entrepreneurial team of "Agriculture Dreams Come True" of Nankai University, picking jujubes together with jujube farmers in Shanxi, and helping them increase income through e-commerce

Photo by Nie Jici

玑瑛青年公社 3D 打印团队

王晓明 摄

3D Printing Team of the Ji Ying Youth Commune

Photo by Wang Xiaoming

南开大学研究生支教团服务西部 20 年，累计派遣支教队员
223 人。图为正在西藏拉萨达孜中心小学支教的同学

常小松　摄

The support teaching team of the Graduate School of Nankai University has
served the western region for 20 years and has dispatched 223 members of the
support teaching team. The picture shows students who are teaching at the Lhasa
Dazi Central Primary School in Tibet

Photo by Chang Xiaosong

无人值守自助找零的诚信超市
王晓明 摄

Integrity supermarket with unattended self-service changing
Photo by Wang Xiaoming

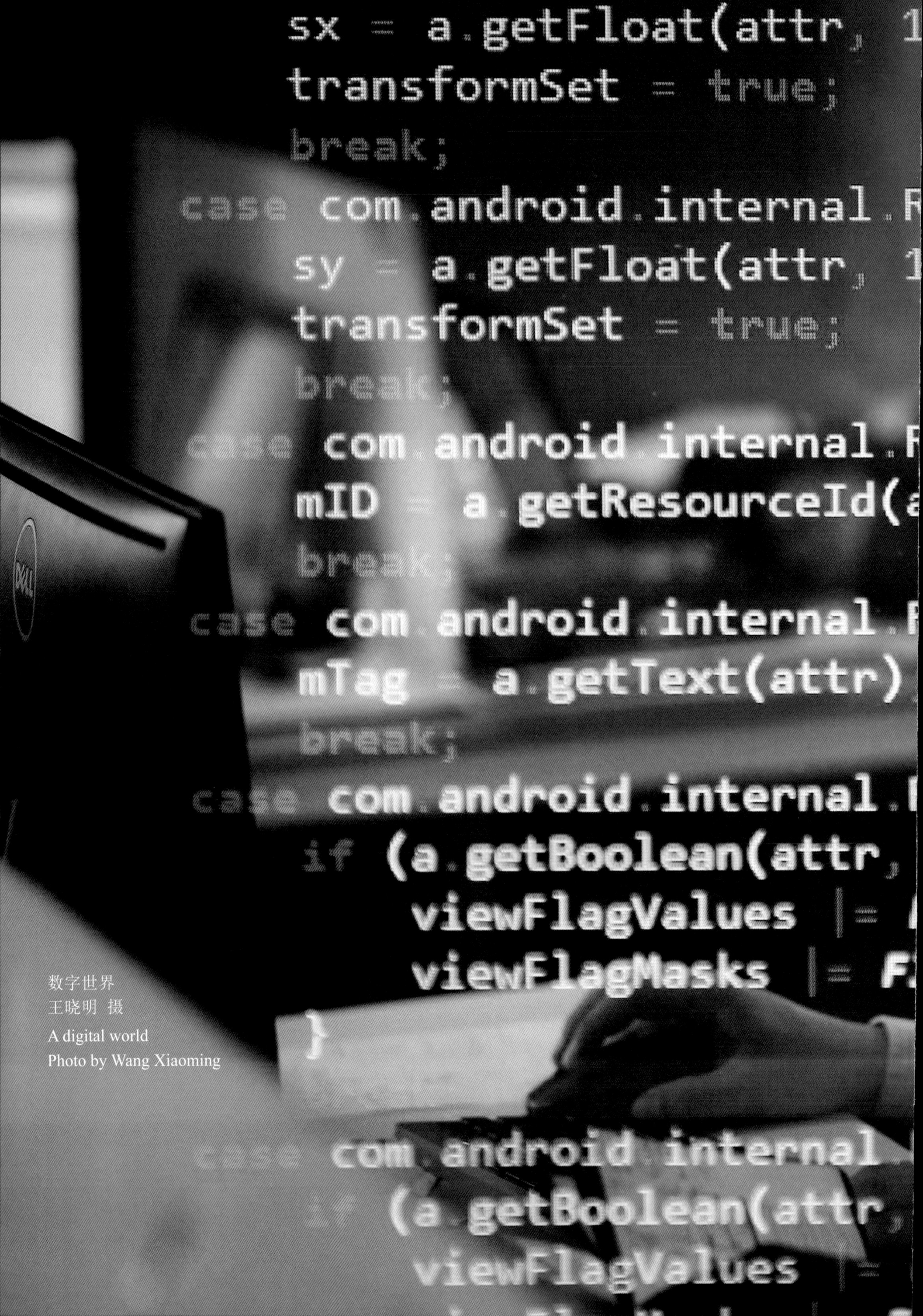

数字世界
王晓明 摄
A digital world
Photo by Wang Xiaoming

```
styleable.View_scaleY:

styleable.View_id:
r, NO_ID);

styleable.View_tag:

styleable.View_fitsSystemWindows:
lse)) {
TS_SYSTEM_WINDOWS
S_SYSTEM_WINDOWS

styleable.View_focusable:
lse)) {
CUSABLE
```

文学院数字中国画实验室 3D 打印中国风版擎天柱
吴军辉 摄

3D printing a Chinese version of Optimus Prime printed by the
Digital Chinese Painting Laboratory of the School of Literature
Photo by Wu Junhui

第四章 逐孤勇

Courage to Fight Alone

"一生只做一件事"，这是数学大师陈省身送给青年人的箴言。从 20 岁入数学之门到 93 岁逝世，陈省身专心数学七十余年。在数学人眼中，一支笔可以运算出万事万物的规律，一块黑板便能解开宇宙的奥秘，就能勾勒出如万花筒般的美丽世界。

暮色苍茫看劲松，乱云飞渡仍从容。科学探索也许意味着寂寞。从创校伊始到百年华诞，南开园中总有这样一群矢志科研的人们，在追求真理的道路上，踽踽独行，竞逐孤勇。他们胸怀家国天下，他们兼济百姓苍生，他们锐意进取，他们持之以恒。"吾生有涯知无涯，以中国之名，突破科学认知的边界；面壁半生图破壁，以科学之光，照亮民族复兴的前程。"他们是青春最好的代名词，也正如南开品格，愈难愈开、愈挫愈勇，披荆斩棘，风雨兼程！

"Do only one thing in your life", this is the advice given to young people by the great mathematician Chern Shiing-shen. He had devoted himself to mathematics for more than 70 years, from the age of 20, when he just entered the world of mathematics, to the age of 93, when his life ended. In the eyes of mathematicians, a pen can work out the law of everything, and a blackboard can unravel the mystery of the universe, presenting a beautiful world that dazzles like a kaleidoscope.

Amid the growing shades of dusk stand sturdy pines; riotous clouds sweep past, swift and tranquil. Scientific exploration might bring loneliness. From the founding of NKU to its centennial anniversary, there has always been such a group of people committed to scientific research. On the road of pursuing the truth, they walked in solitude and fight alone. They cherished the fate of the nation and the world, dedicated to people's well-being and determined to move forward with persistence. As the quote goes, "My life has an end, but the pursuit of knowledge has none. In the name of China, I am determined to break the boundaries of scientific cognition. Devoting half of my life to the search of answers, I will use science to illuminate the road of the nation's rejuvenation." Their names are the best synonyms of youth. Their life is also a manifestation of NKU's spirit: go forward despite difficulties, gather courage despite frustrations, find a way through sufferings, and never stop for hardships!

元素有机化学国家重点实验室
姜宝成 摄
The State Key Laboratory of Element-organic Chemistry
Photo by Jiang Baocheng

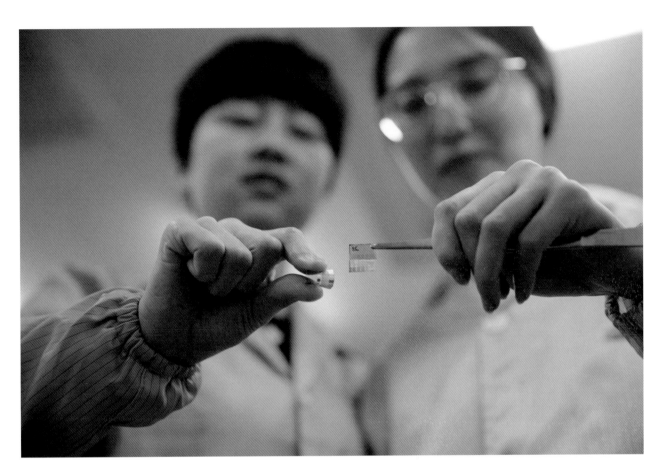

实验人员展示有机太阳能电池柔性特质
吴军辉 摄

Lab staff demonstrating the flexibility property of organic solar cells
Photo by Wu Junhui

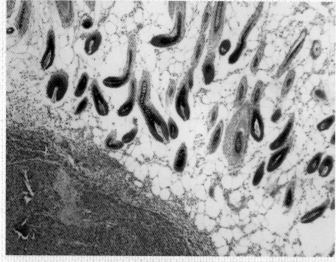

陨石·地球（科学显微摄影）
高　珊　摄
Aerolite·Earth (by microscope)
Photo by Gao Shan

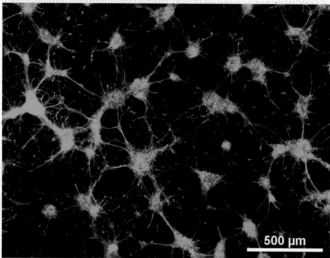

错综复杂的神经网（科学显微摄影）
贾真珍　摄
The intricate neural network (by microscope)
Photo by Jia Zhenzhen

用心发现科研之美——奇妙心形肿瘤细胞
激光共聚焦成像（科学显微摄影）
李　杰　摄
Discover the beauty of scientific research —
marvelous heart-shaped tumor cells by laser
confocal imaging (by microscope)
Photo by Li Jie

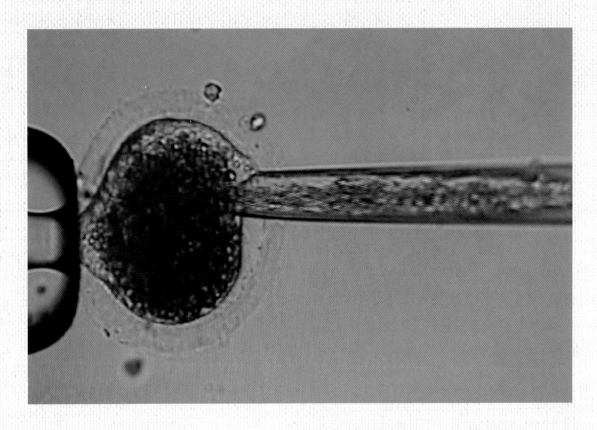

微操作系统显微图
新闻中心资料图
Micro-operating system micrograph
Photo /NKU News Center

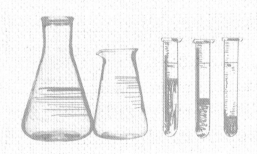

环境科学与工程学院学生在做电化学方法降解染料污水实验
吴军辉 摄

Students from the College of Environmental Science and Engineering conducting
an experiment of using electrochemical method to degrade dye wastewater
Photo by Wu Junhui

环境科学与工程学院学生测试机动车污染实时地图系统
王晓明 摄

Students from the College of Environmental Science and Engineering
testing the real-time motor vehicle pollution map system
Photo by Wang Xiaoming

科研人员正在测试脑控汽车
姜宝成 摄
Researchers testing a brain-controlled car
Photo by Jiang Baocheng

脑控机器人投掷垃圾
王晓明 摄

Brain-controlled robot dropping garbage
Photo by Wang Xiaoming

人工智能学院学生正在测试蛇形机器人

姜宝成 摄

Students from the AI College testing a snake like robot

Photo by Jiang Baocheng

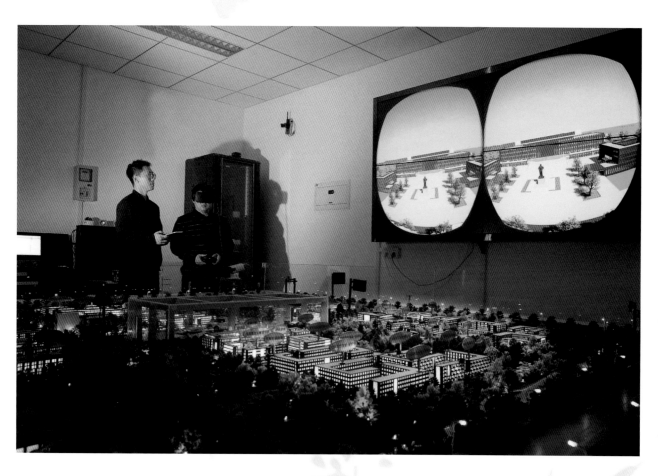

引入 VR 系统的物联网技术
吴军辉 摄
Internet of Things technology with a VR system
Photo by Wu Junhui

医学院学生正在检查斑马鱼生长情况
聂际慈 摄
Students from the School of Medicine checking the growth situation of zebra fish
Photo by Nie Jici

药物化学生物学国家重点实验室内的科研主题春联
吴军辉 摄

Spring Festival Couplets with the theme of the State
Laboratory of Medical Chemical Biology
Photo by Wu Junhui

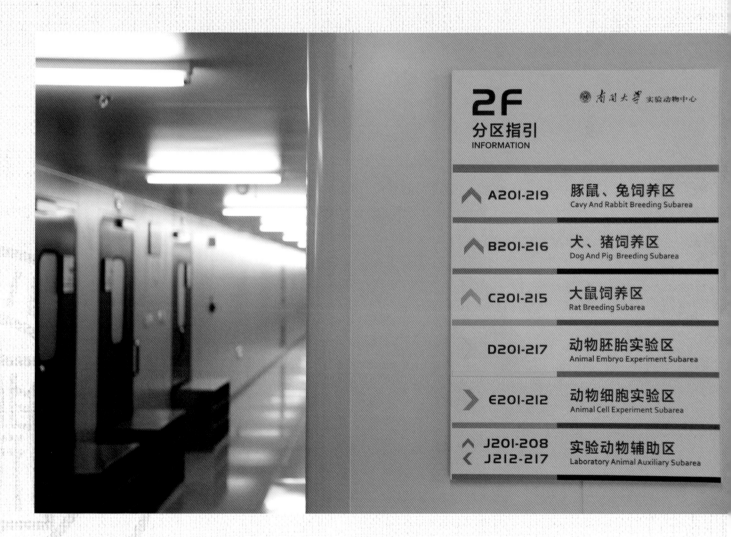

南开大学实验动物中心投用，服务京津冀，辐射华北地区
吴军辉 摄

Nankai University Laboratory Animal Center put into use,
serving Beijing-Tianjin-Hebei and the larger North China area
Photo by Wu Junhui

学生科研团队研发净水发电
王晓明 摄

The students research team working on hydroelectricity
Photo by Wang Xiaoming

科研人员展示二氧化碳瓶中的"可呼吸电池"
工晓明 摄

Researchers demonstrating the "respirable battery" in a carbon
dioxide bottle
Photo by Wang Xiaoming

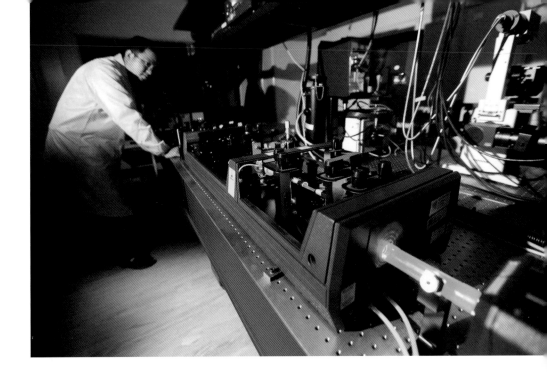

现代光学研究所研究人员调试 Z 扫描系统
吴军辉 摄

Researchers from the Institute of Modern Optics commissioning
the Z-scan system
Photo by Wu Junhui

研究人员正在操作激光扫描共聚焦显微镜
吴军辉 摄

Researchers operating the Confocal Laser Scanning Microscope
Photo by Wu Junhui

植物污水发电
王晓明 摄
Plant-enhanced sewage power generation
Photo by Wang Xiaoming

实验人员正在使用高效液相色谱仪纯化多肽
吴军辉 摄

Lab staff using the high performance liquid chromatography
to purify polypeptide
Photo by Wu Junhui

生命科学学院学生正在观察转基因番茄长势
吴军辉 摄

Students from the College of Life Science observing the growth
situation of transgenic tomato
Photo by Wu Junhui

电子信息与光学工程学院实验室
吴军辉 摄

A laboratory at the College of Electronic information and Optical Engineering
Photo by Wu Junhui

专注科研的南开人
聂际慈 摄

Nankai people dedicated to scientific research
Photo by Nie Jici

来自海内外的 27 名院士汇聚南开
李 想 摄
27 academicians from home and abroad gathering together
Photo by Li Xiang

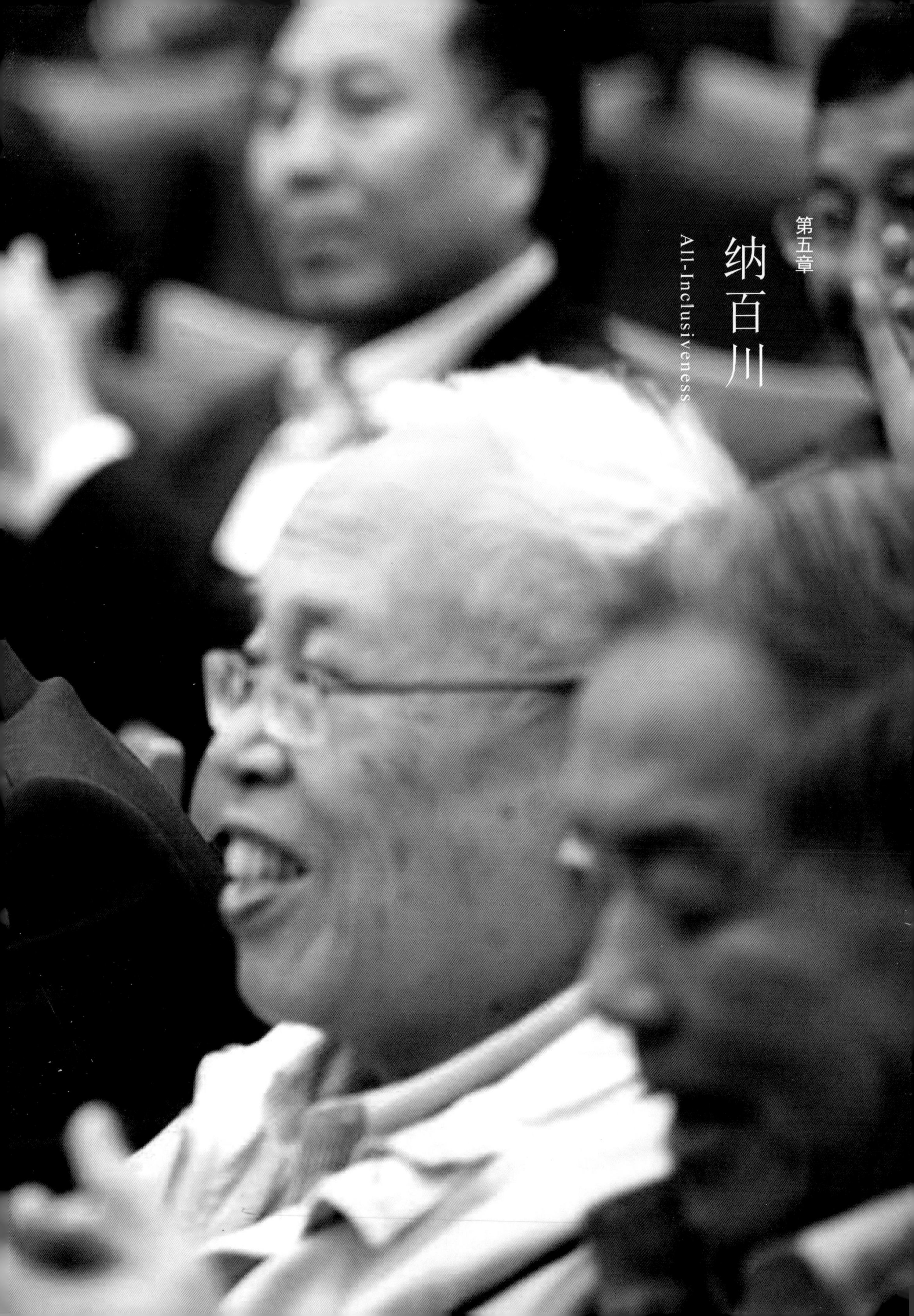

第五章

纳百川

All-Inclusiveness

留学生过春节
高　鹏　摄
Overseas student celebrating the Spring Festival
Photo by Gao Peng

第五章 纳百川

Chapter V All-Inclusiveness

南开校徽呈八角形，由两枚正方形叠加变换而来，既取"方方正正做人"之意，也蕴含日新月异的南开大学"面向四面八方，胸怀博大，广纳新知，锐意进取"之精神。从借鉴西方经验创办中国现代大学，到经历"土洋之争"后决心扎根中国，再到如今海纳百川、兼收并蓄，进而与世界一流大学携手共进、同台竞技……

"文明新旧能相益，心理东西本自同。"国际化的南开因文明互鉴变得更加多彩，而世界各国文化的交融，也让这座百年学府更加富有朝气与活力。教学楼里，外籍教师们各放异彩而又美美与共；课堂之上，中国传统文化让外国学生赞叹博大精深；运动场上，留学生激扬汗水绽放青春笑脸；毕业典礼，中外同学一起分享喜悦、其乐融融……东西文化交流、国际"大咖"来访讲学、携手世界顶尖高校开展联合研究、学生培养，这方国际化的校园为南开人拓宽了梦想的舞台，也让中国传统文化从这里走向世界。一幅新时代"全球南开"的壮丽图卷正在世界的东方徐徐展开！

The emblem of the Nankai University is in octagon, which overlaid and combined by two squares. It takes the meaning of "be a person of integrity", and the spirit of Nankai, a university that progresses with each passing day, "opens to all sides and new knowledge, and always forges ahead". From drawing on the western experience to establish a modern Chinese university, to the "the dispute between local and foreign style" before the determination to take root in China, Nankai has evolved into a university with inclusive and all-embracing spirit which now cooperates and competes with world-class universities.

"The old and new civilizations can draw on each other, and the east and west mindsets are fundamentally the same." Nankai University, with its international vision, has become more diversified from the exchanges between civilizations and the blending of cultures of all countries, which has in turn made this century-old university more vital and energetic. In teaching buildings, international teachers excel at their work and learn from each other. In classrooms, international students admire the profound traditional Chinese culture. On sports field, overseas students demonstrate their energy and youth in sweat and with smile. At Commencements, Chinese and foreign students share joy and happiness in perfect harmony. Through programs such as east and west cultural exchanges, lectures by international renowned scholars, as well as joint research and student training projects in cooperation with the world's top universities, this international campus has broadened the stage for Nankai students to pursue their dreams, and also brings traditional Chinese culture to the international arena. A magnificent scene of a "Global Nankai" in the new era is unfolding in the east of the world!

世界工程组织联合会（WFEO）前主席马尔万·阿卜杜勒·哈米德南开讲学
吴军辉 摄

A lecture by Marwan Abdel Hamid, former chairman of the World Federation of
Engineering Organizations (WFEO) at Nankai University
Photo by Wu Junhui

美国科学院院士丹尼尔·波特诺伊南开讲学
吴军辉 摄

A Lecture by Daniel Portnoy, a member of the American Academy of Sciences at Nankai University
Photo by Wu Junhui

国际数学联盟秘书长马丁·格瑞切尔

吴军辉 摄

Martin Grötschel, Secretary of the International Mathematical Union

Photo by Wu Junhui

诺贝尔经济学奖得主、美国哈佛大学教授埃里克·马斯金南开讲学
姜宝成 摄

A lecture by Nobel Laureate in Economic Science, Harvard University professor Eric Maskin at Nankai University
Photo by Jiang Baocheng

诺贝尔化学奖得主、著名化学家、碳 60 发现者罗伯特·科尔受聘
南开大学客座教授
游思行 摄

Robert F.Curl, winner of the Nobel Laureate in Chemistry for the discovery of the nanomaterial buckminsterfullerene and a famous chemist, conferred as guest professor of Nankai University
Photo by You Sihang

美国化学家雷·鲍曼院士受聘南开大学杨石先讲座教授
姜宝成 摄

American chemist Ray H.Baughman, a member of the NAE, employed by Nankai
University as Yang Shixian Chair Professor
Photo by Jiang Baocheng

美国著名计量经济学家、诺贝尔经济学经获得者罗伯特·恩格尔
受聘南开大学名誉教授
王晓明 摄

Robert Engel, a well-known econometrician and Nobel Laureate in Economic Science,
employed by Nankai University as an honorary professor
Photo by Wang Xiaoming

时任新加坡总统陈庆炎获南开大学名誉博士
吴军辉 摄

The then Singaporean President Chen Qingyan
received an honorary doctorate from Nankai
University
Photo by Wu Junhui

英国驻华大使吴百纳受聘南开大学客座教授
张道正 摄

Dame Barbara Janet Woodward, the British
Ambassador to China, employed by Nankai
University as guest professor
Photo by Zhang Daozheng

时任意大利驻华大使白达宁南开演讲
王晓明 摄

A speech by the then Italian ambassador to China
Alberto Bradanini at Nankai University
Photo by Wang Xiaoming

美国前防长威廉·科恩南开讲座
姜宝成 摄

A lecture by the former US Defense Secretary
William Cohen at Nankai University
Photo by Jiang Baocheng

欧盟委员会前主席、意大利前总理、南开大学名誉教授
罗马诺·普罗迪做客天津论坛
姜宝成 摄

Romano Prodi, Former President of the European Commission,
former Prime Minister of Italy, honorary Professor of Nankai
University, at the Tianjin Forum as a guest
Photo by Jiang Baocheng

法国前外长洛朗·法比尤斯南开演讲
王晓明 摄

A speech by French former Minister of Foreign
Affairs Laurent Fabius
Photo by Wang Xiaoming

世界经济论坛主席克劳斯·施瓦布获南开大学名誉博士
游思行 摄

Klaus Schwab, Executive President of the World Economic Forum,
received an honorary doctorate from Nankai University
Photo by You Sihang

意大利总统文化顾问路易斯·高塔特受聘
南开大学客座教授
吴军辉 摄

Louis Godart, Director for the Conservation of
Artistic Heritage of the Italian President conferred
as Honorary Guest Professor of Nankai University
Photo by Wu Junhui

美国著名石油大亨洛克菲勒的后代洛克菲勒二世和洛克菲勒三世来到南开大学，参观了洛克菲勒捐建的南开大学思源堂并与大学生交流
姜宝成 摄

Rockefeller II and Rockefeller III, the descendants of the famous American oil industry magnate Rockefeller, came to Nankai University to visit the Siyuan Hall of Nankai University donated by Rockefeller and communicated with the students.
Photo by Jiang Baocheng

NBA 退役球星诺姆·尼克松与南开学生互动
韦承金 摄
NBA retired player Norm Nixon interacting with Nankai students
Photo by Wei Chengjin

留学生运动会
王晓明 摄

Overseas Students Games
Photo by Wang Xiaoming

中外学生交流剪纸与动漫
刘瑞麒 摄

Chinese and foreign students exchanging ideas and
works of paper cutting and animation
Photo by Liu Ruiqi

留学生表演中华武术
游思行 摄

Overseas students performing Chinese martial arts
Photo by You Sihang

一名留学生展示他制作的香囊
王晓明 摄

An overseas student demonstrating the sachet he made
Photo by Wang Xiaoming

留学生运动会
游思行 摄
Overseas Students Games
Photo by You Sihang

清明放纸鸢
游思行 摄
Kite flying on the Tomb Sweeping Day
Photo by You Sihang

中英首个联合研究生院、南开大学－格拉斯哥大学联合研究
生院首届学生获中英双学位
聂际慈 摄

The first joint graduate school between China and the UK and the first
class of graduate students of Nankai University-Glasgow University Joint
Graduate School conferred a China-UK dual degree
Photo by Nie Jici

外籍师生联欢会
姜宝成 摄
Foreign teachers and students having a party
Photo by Jiang Baocheng

留学生包饺子
姜宝成 摄
Overseas students making Jiao Zi (Chinese dumpling)
Photo by Jiang Baocheng

热爱相声的美国女孩陆梦生
姜宝成 摄
American girl Lu Mengsheng who loves cross talk
Photo by Jiang Baocheng

"一带一路"外籍学生招聘会
姜宝成 摄
"Belt and Road" foreign students' job fair
Photo by Jiang Baocheng

新开湖畔中外学生一起交流
游思行 摄
Exchanges between Chinese and foreign students by
the Xinkai Lake
Photo by You Sihang

留学生接受安全教育
刘东岳 摄
Overseas students at a safety orientation
Photo by Liu Dongyue

南开大学学生合唱团西班牙国际合唱大赛夺冠
田 雨 摄
Nankai University Student Choir won the first place in the Spanish
International Choir Competition

"粽"情端午节
刘东岳 摄

Enjoying Zong Zi (traditional Chinese rice-pudding) on the Dragon Boat Festival
Photo by Liu Dongyue

留学生表演京东大鼓
沈 岳 摄

International students performing Jingdong Da Gu (an art form of drum
music and recitative, performed in the East Beijing dialect)
Photo by Shen Yue

外教与幼儿园小朋友做游戏

王晓明　摄

Foreign teachers playing with kindergarten kids

Photo by Wang Xiaoming

留学生的毕业季
高 鹏 摄

The graduation season for overseas students
Photo by Gao Peng

公益晨跑·资助贫困小学生
游思行 摄
A public welfare morning run to fund primary school students
Photo by You Sihang

第六章

Never Left

南离开

意见箱

八里台校区学二食堂一角
张树楠 摄
A corner of the 2nd student canteen at the Balitai Campus
Photo by Zang Shunan

第六章·南离开
Never Left

还记得历尽千辛踏进南开校园那一刻的心情吗？还记得从初入校园的迷茫到决心立公增能、学以报国的蜕变吗？还记得为铭记国耻校耻而鸣响的校钟吗？还记得敬献给南开先贤、革命烈士、前辈学人的鲜花吗？还记得同寝室的兄弟或姐妹，一起读书一起玩耍一起游历名山大川吗？还记得为撰写论文亦或实验攻关而夜以继日吗？还记得那些年听过的音乐会、讲座，参加过的社会实践吗？还记得招聘会现场那长得看不到首尾的队伍吗？还记得那年夏天不为赚钱只为情怀的"跳蚤市场"吗？还记得毕业晚会燃情互动的狂欢吗？还记得毕业典礼结束后和好友相拥而泣的泪水吗？

"在南开学习是一件幸福的事！"百年风雨路，一生南开情。南开给万千学子筑起逐梦的舞台，也给万千校友留下了一份家的牵挂。聚是一团火，散作满天星，这里是青春的储藏地，有关青春的故事永远未完待续。

Do you still remember the moment when you stepped into the campus of Nankai after all the painstaking effort you have made? Do you still remember the transformation from the confusion when first entering the university to the determination to dedicate to public interest, enhance all-round capability and contribute what is leant to the country? Do you still remember the school bell that tolls for the national and school humiliation? Do you still remember the flowers dedicated to the past Nankai scholars, revolutionary martyrs and alumni? Do you still remember reading, playing, and travelling around the famous mountains and great waters with your roommates? Do you still remember working day and night to write a paper or tackle a research problem? Do you still remember the concerts, lectures and social practice activities that you have attended in those years? Do you still remember the line at the job fair that was too long to see the end? Do you still remember the "flea market" in that summer that wasn't for making money but for feeling the moment? Do you still remember the passion and hilarity at the graduation party? Do you still remember hugging your friends and weeping together after the Commencement?

"It was happy to study in Nankai!" A hundred-year's trek of the university has given us a lifetime of loving memory. Nankai has set up a stage for a myriad of students to pursue their dreams and has become a home for thousands of homesick alumni. We came together forming a fire and left as countless sparks. Here it houses our youth, and here our youth continues.

高招进行时　熙熙攘攘的大中路
王晓明　摄
College enrollment ongoing　the bustling Dazhong road
Photo by Wang Xiaoming

欢迎你，新同学
吴军辉　摄
Welcome, freshmen
Photo by Wu Junhui

开学啦
游思行 摄

A new term begins
Photo by You Sihang

众里寻他千百度
游思行 摄

A thousand times or more in quest of one
Photo by You Sihang

写给未来
王晓明 摄

A letter to future
Photo by Wang Xiaoming

我在南开等你来！
吴军辉 摄

I'm waiting for you at Nankai University!
Photo by Wu Junhui

学校为身高超过 190cm 的学生定制加长床铺
吴军辉 摄

The university custom-made extra-long beds for students over 190cm in height
Photo by Wu Junhui

作家王蒙做客南开名家讲坛
姜宝成 摄
Writer Wang Meng at Celebrity
Forum as a guest
Photo by Jiang Baocheng

作家白先勇做客南开
姜宝成 摄
Writer Bai Xianyong at Nankai
Photo by Jiang Baocheng

故宫文物修复师王津南开分
享"工匠精神"
吴军辉　摄
Wang Jin, a Palace Museum cultural
relics restorer, sharing his view on
"The Spirit of Craftsman" at Nankai
University
Photo by Wu Junhui

经济学家、北京大学教授林毅夫做客天津论坛
姜宝成 摄

Economist and Peking University professor Lin
Yifu at the Tianjin Forum as a guest
Photo by Jiang Baocheng

郭明义爱心团队结缘南开人
沈　岳摄
Guo Mingyi Loving Care Team formed
ties with Nankai People
Photo by Shen Yue

诗人席慕蓉南开演讲"父亲的
草原母亲的河"
吴军辉摄
Poet Xi Murong giving a speech on "Father's
Grassland and Mother's River" at Nankai University
Photo by Wu Junhui

大型原创话剧《杨石先》
吴军辉 摄
Large-scale original stage play "Yang Shixian"
Photo by Wu Junhui

拼搏
任永华 摄
Fight for it
Photo by Ren Yonghua

"校长杯"足球赛瞬间
吴军辉 摄
A moment at the "President's Cup" Football Game
Photo by Wu Junhui

"校长杯"篮球赛决赛瞬间
吴军辉 摄

A moment at the final of the "President's Cup" Basketball Game
Photo by Wu Junhui

飞跃
林坤洋 摄

A leap
Photo by Lin Kunyang

花式跳绳
吴军辉 摄
Figure rope-skipping
Photo by Wu Junhui

南开大学啦啦队庆祝夺冠
高 鹏 摄
Nankai University cheerleaders
celebrating the championship
Photo by Gao Peng

南开大学承办第六届东亚运动会排球项目
吴军辉 摄
Nankai University hosted the Volleyball
games of the 6th East Asian Games
Photo by Wu Junhui

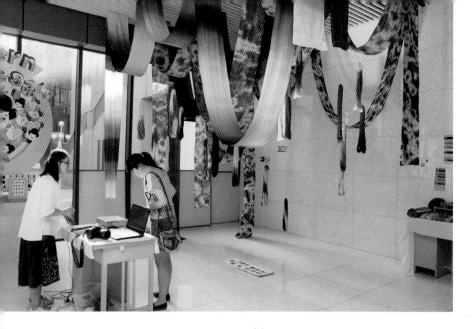

畅游艺术海洋
任永华 摄

Enjoying a dive into the ocean of art
Photo by Ren Yonghua

人文雅舍陶铸公能品格
吴军辉 摄

Well-mannered students in elegantly managed dorms manifesting the character of "Dedication to public interests and acquisition of all-round capability"
Photo by Wu Junhui

老图前的舞者
高 鹏 摄

Dancers in front of the Old Library
Photo by Gao Peng

南开大学首届跨年演唱会现场
吴军辉　摄

The First Nankai University New
Year Concert

Photo by Wu Junhui

新年音乐会上南开大学学生合
唱团与学生交响乐团联袂表演
吴军辉　摄

Nankai University Student Choir
and Student Symphony Orchestra
performing together at the New
Year Concert

Photo by Wu Junhui

南开大学梨园春会
张　立摄

The spring gathering at Liyuan Garden in Nankai University
Photo by Zhang Li

两名新生在迎水道校区大礼堂参观
游思行　摄

Two freshmen visiting the Auditorium at the Yingshuidao Campus
Photo by You Sihang

新校区宿舍楼内的共享厨房
游思行 摄

Shared kitchen in the new campus dormitory
Photo by You Sihang

小小一卡通　浓浓母校情
吴军辉 摄

A small campus card stores the deepest care
and love of the Alma Mater
Photo by Wu Junhui

点滴文明 从我做起
游思行 摄

Civilized behaviors start with small things with everyone
Photo by You Sihang

爱心传递现场两名学生"满载而归"，该活动旨在旧物分享，减少浪费
游思行 摄

Two students returning fully loaded from the site of the "Loving Pass-on" program
which aims to share old things and reduce waste
Photo by You Sihang

南开学子拾金不昧
吴军辉 摄
Nankai students returned money found
Photo by Wu Junhui

庆"三八"南开学子为宿管阿姨送枝花
聂际慈 摄
Nankai students gave flowers to female dorm administrators
in celebration of the International Women's Day
Photo by Nie Jici

我们毕业啦
林坤洋 摄
We graduated!
Photo by Lin Kunyang

毕业生手绘南开主题明信片献礼母校
李　想　摄

Graduate hand-painted a Nankai theme postcard as a
gift to the Alma Mater
Photo by Li Xiang

开往未来
游思行　摄

A drive into future
Photo by You Sihang

高　鹏 摄
含辛茹苦

Bearing hardships
Photo by Gao Peng

分享喜悦
吴军辉 摄
Sharing the joy
Photo by Wu Junhui

毕业季的泪水
吴军辉 摄

Tears in the graduation season
Photo by Wu Junhui

接受"拨穗礼"的毕业生
吴军辉 摄

Graduates at the "turning of the tassel" ceremony
Photo by Wu Junhui

毕业典礼上"跑旗"的女生
吴军辉 摄

A flag-bearing girl running at the Commencement
Photo by Wu Junhui

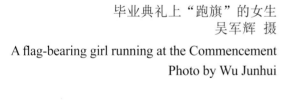

"研"途不易
吴军辉 摄
A tough journey of research
Photo by Wu Junhui

毕业生的"跳蚤市场"
游思行 摄
Graduates' "Flea Market"
Photo by You Sihang

艺术设计系毕业生展示毕业作品
吴军辉 摄

Graduates of the Department of Art and Design demonstrating their graduation works
Photo by Wu Junhui

排球场上的毕业留影
高　鹏 摄

Graduation photo on the volleyball court
Photo by Gao Peng

激情四射的毕业晚会
游思行 摄
An exuberant graduation party
Photo by You Sihang

毕业不散场
游思行 摄
Graduation is not the end
Photo by You Sihang

爱你 99　南开大学集体婚礼
王晓明 摄

Love you 99　A group wedding at
Nankai University
Photo by Wang Xiaoming

最美青春在南开
姜宝成 摄

The most beautiful youth at Nankai
Photo by Jiang Baocheng

国家一级演员、1950 届校友鲁园在母校毕业典礼上深情朗诵

吴军辉 摄

The soulful recitation by Lu Yuan, a national Class A actress and 1950 alumna,
at the Commencement of the Alma Mater

Photo by Wu Junhui

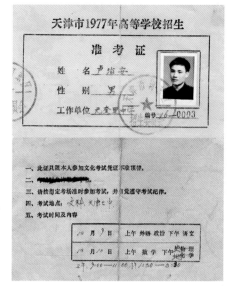

1977 年高考准考证
游思行 摄

admission tickets of the 1977 college
entrance examination
Photo by You Sihang

1977 级考生重返校园：感谢那年的高考
游思行 摄

1977 college candidates returned to the campus:
thanks to the college entrance examination that year
Photo by You Sihang

南开大学 1977 级毕业生留影
游思行 摄

Nankai University 1977 graduates taking a picture
Photo by You Sihang

"归来仍是少年" 1979级数学系校友
张文中在母校开学典礼上捐赠1亿元
史 嵩摄

"A boy as he was when returning to the Alma Mater"
Zhang Wenzhong, a 1979 alumnus of the Department
of Mathematics, donated 100 million yuan at the term
opening ceremony of his Alma Mater
Photo by Shi Song

1988级数学系校友吴慧龙登顶珠峰
范 波摄

Wu Huilong, a 1988 alumnus of the Department of
Mathematics, reached the summit of Mount Everest
Photo by Fan Bo

1990 级国经贸系校友李健民登顶
珠峰并展开南开旗帜
多吉次仁 摄

Li Jianmin, a 1990 alumnus of the National Economic
and Trade Department, reached the summit of Mount
Everest holding the Nankai Banner.
Photo by Dogi Tshiren

南以离开
王晓明 摄

Hard to leave NKU
Photo by Wang Xiaoming

南开师生摆出"我爱中国"字样献礼祖国 70 华诞
张剑影、吕　军　摄
Nankai faculty and students line up to form the Chinese characters of
"I love China" to commemorate the 70th birthday of the motherland
Photo by Zhang Jianying& Lyu Jun

第七章

新百年

A New Century

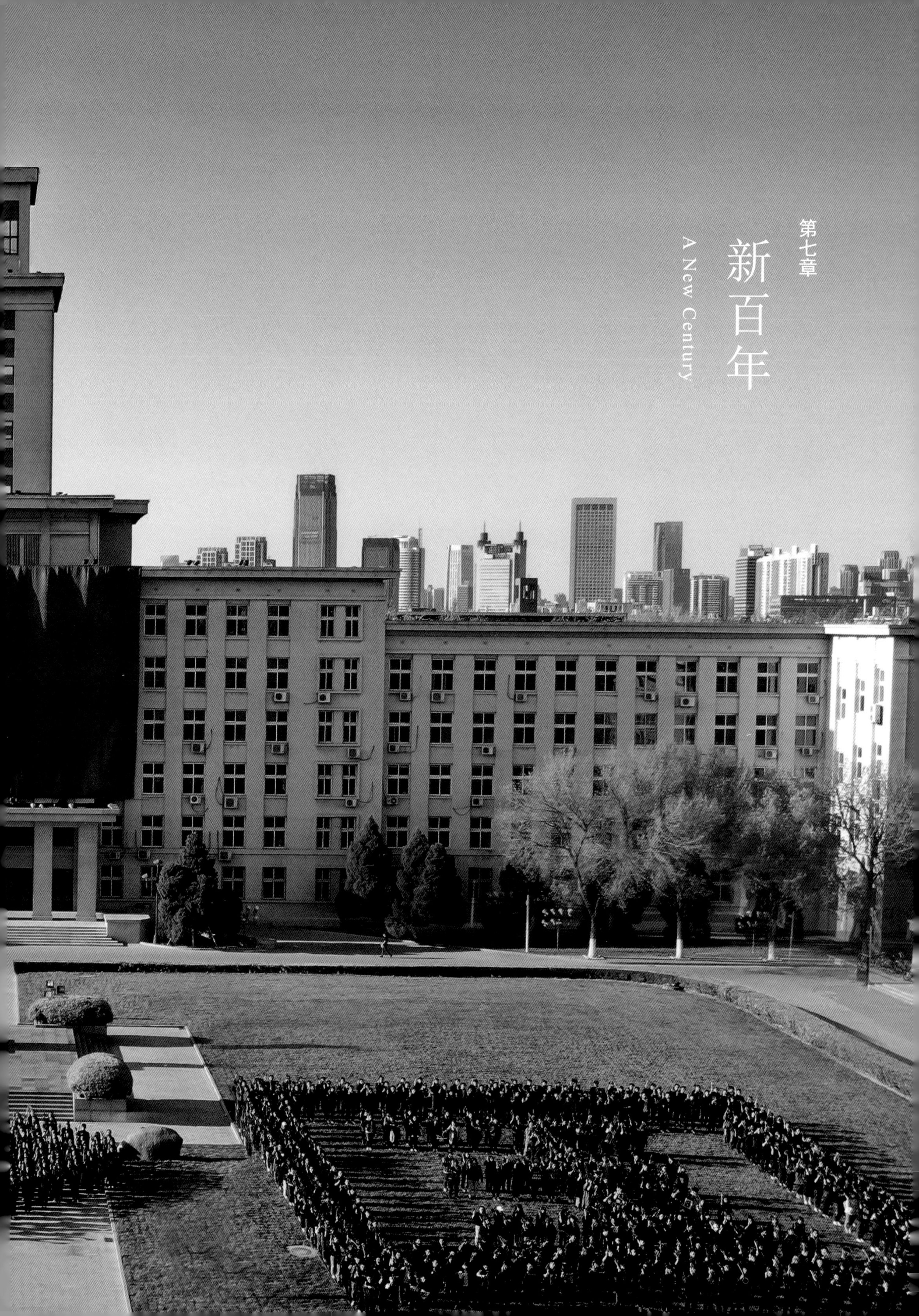

蓝图实现
吴军辉 摄

Implementation of the blueprint
Photo by Wu Junhui

第七章 新百年
Chapter VII A New Century

巍巍南开允公能，百年芳华更日新！百年南开，走出了心系国家、服务社会的爱国道路，铸就了"允公允能、日新月异"的"公能"品格，焕发出充满朝气、面向未来的青春精神。这是南开最深厚的历史积淀，也是南开自信自强的底气！

汲汲骎骎、月异日新，发煌我前途无垠……在南开的青春里，始终有着关于成长的梦想，不停探索，不断追寻；在南开的青春里，始终有颗关于为国育才的初心，不停闪动，不懈拼搏。十秩峥嵘薪火相传，百年恰是风华正茂。新世纪、新希望、新百年、新篇章，南开人正以昂扬的姿态，脚踏实地、仰望星空、勇敢追梦，奋力书写下一个百年的青春华章！

A hundred years later, this lofty university that has served the public interests and honed its students' capabilities is innovating as ever! In the past 100 years, it has explored a patriotic road of caring for the country and serving the society, hammered out the devoted character of "Dedication to public interests, acquisition of all-round capability, and aspiration for progress with each passing day ", and has been glowing with a vibrant, youthful and future-oriented spirit. Those are the most profound historical accumulation of Nankai and the very source of its self-confidence and self-reliance!

Run at a gallop to improve with each passing day and open up the boundless future ... In Nankai's youthful days, it has been constantly exploring and pursuing the dream of growth; in Nankai's youthful days, it has been fighting unremittingly for its original aspiration of fostering talent for the country. Ten extraordinary decades have ushered the university into its prime time. In the new century and with new hopes, we open the new chapter into the next one hundred years. The high-spirited Nankai people are looking up at the stars while keeping their feet on the ground. They are bravely chasing their dreams, through which they will write a great new chapter of the next century!

建设中的新校区项目，图为综合业务东楼施工现场
吴军辉 摄

The new campus project under construction. The photo shows the
construction site of the East Wing of General Affairs Building
Photo by Wu Junhui

建设中的新校区项目，图为文科组团施工现场
新闻中心资料图

The new campus project under construction. The photo shows the
construction site of the liberal arts group
Photo /NKU News Center

鸟瞰郁郁葱葱的新校区
张哲浩 摄

An aerial view of the lush new campus
Photo by Zhang Zhehao

2015 年 9 月 5 日津南校区正式启用，图为披红挂彩的搬迁车辆
游思行 摄

The Jinnan Campus officially opened on September 5th, 2015. The photo shows
the relocation vehicles with colorful decorations.
Photo by You Sihang

2015 年 9 月 5 日津南校区正式启用，图为师生在新地标前合影
游思行 摄

The Jinnan Campus officially opened on September 5th, 2015. The photo shows
the faculty and students taking photos in front of the new landmark.
Photo by You Sihang

坦阔的图书馆南广场成为学校大型活动的良好场地
吴军辉 摄
The spacious square to the south of the library is a great venue for
large school events
Photo by Wu Junhui

崭新图书馆营造舒适阅读环境
林坤洋 摄

The brand-new library creates a comfortable reading environment
Photo by Lin Kunyang

新校区图书馆工具书阅览区
吴军辉 摄

Reading area of tool books at the new campus library
Photo by Wu Junhui

大通学生中心大剧场
吴军辉 摄

Grand Theatre of the Datong Student Center
Photo by Wu Junhui

新校区图书馆顶层玻璃幕墙
姜宝成 摄

Top glass curtain wall of the new campus library
Photo by Jiang Baocheng

蓝天下的图书馆和周恩来总理塑像
吴军辉 摄
Statue of the Prime Minister Zhou Enlai in front of the library under the blue sky
Photo by Wu Junhui

夜幕下的"海棠花"学生中心流光溢彩
姜丙骏 摄
The "Begonia Flower" Student Center at night is full of brilliance
Photo by Jiang Bingjun

南开师生歌唱祖国献礼新中国 70 华诞
姜丙骏 摄

Nankai faculty and students singing for the motherland to
commemorate the 70th birthday of the new China
Photo by Jiang Bingjun

百年校庆吉祥物阳阳和亮亮
张 立 摄
Yang Yang and Liang Liang, the centennial celebration mascots
Photo by Zhang Li

百年南开 爱你不变
王晓明 摄

Love unchanged for Naikai University in one hundred years
Photo by Wang Xiaoming

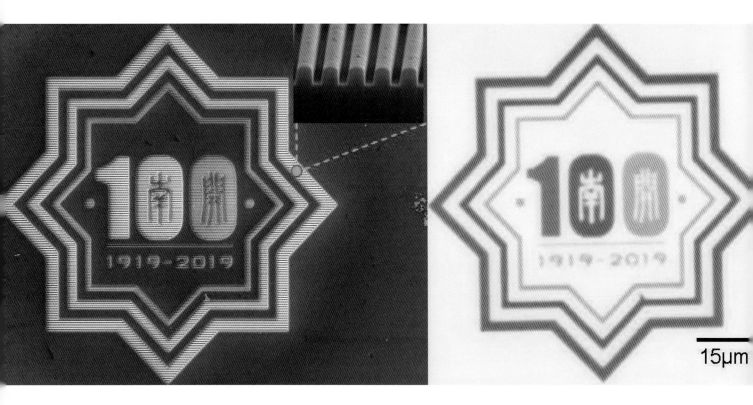

15μm

南开大学团队攻克铌酸锂微加工世界难题，在发丝
粗细的铌酸锂材料上"雕刻"出百年校庆Logo
任梦昕　摄

A team of Nankai University has solved the world-level challenge of
micromachining lithium niobate, and "carved" the centennial celebration
logo on the hairline lithium niobate material
Photo by Ren Mengxin

百年校庆倒计时 365 天　学生拍摄纪念封
王晓明　摄

365-day countdown for the university centennial celebration;
Students taking photos for the commemorative envelope
Photo by Wang Xiaoming

中国篮协主席、亚洲篮协主席姚明出席
张伯苓体育思想高峰论坛并作主旨演讲
吴军辉 摄

Yao Ming,the president of the Chinese Basketball Association
(CBA) and the chairman of the International Basketball Federation
(FIBA) Asia,attends the Summit of the Forum on Zhang
Boling's Sports Thought and delivers a keynote speech at Nankai
University.
Photo by Wu Junhui

校友"半马"奔向新百年
王晓明 摄
The alumni half-marathon held to usher in the new century
Photo by Wang Xiaoming

中国科学院院士任咏华做客百年南开大讲堂
吴军辉 摄

Ren Yonghua, Academician of the Chinese
Academy of Sciences, at the Centennial Nankai
Lecture as a guest
Photo by Wu Junhui

中国科学院院士张学敏做客百年南开大讲堂
吴军辉 摄

Zhang Xuemin, Academician of the Chinese
Academy of Sciences, at the Centennial Nankai
Lecture as a guest
Photo by Wu Junhui

国际科学理事会全球科学政策特使
弗莱维娅·施莱格尔做客百年南开大讲堂
吴军辉 摄

Flavia Schlegel, Special Envoy for Global Science
Policy of the International Science Council, at the
Centennial Nankai Lecture as a guest
Photo by Wu Junhui

英国医学科学院院士、美国科学促进协会院士、英国皇家学会院士安妮·奥加拉做客百年南开大讲堂
韦承金 摄

Anne O'Garra , Academician of the Academy of Medical Sciences of the United Kingdom , Fellow of the American Association for the Advancement of Science, and a member of the Royal Society of the United Kingdom, at the Centennial Nankai Lecture
Photo by Wei Chengjin

瑞典皇家科学院院士安德斯·利尔加斯做客百年南开大讲堂
吴军辉 摄

Anders Lilgas, Academician of the Royal Swedish Academy of Sciences, at the Centennial Nankai Lecture as a guest
Photo by Wu Junhui

诺贝尔生理或医学奖获得者、中国工程院外籍院士、中国政府友谊奖获得者巴里·詹姆斯·马歇尔做客百年南开大讲堂
吴军辉 摄

Barry James Marshall, winner of the Nobel Prize in Physiology or Medicine, a foreign academician of the Chinese Academy of Engineering , and winner of the Chinese Government Friendship Award , at the Centennial Nankai Lecture as a guest
Photo by Wu Junhui

木斋馆、思源堂、秀山堂在新校区
复建赓续南开文脉
姜丙骏 摄
The Muzhai Museum, Siyuan Hall and Xiushan Hall being
rebuilt at the new campus to carry on Nankai's culture tradition
Photo by Jiang Bingjun

摄影者名录
Directory of Photographers

王俊峰
南开大学媒体校友
Wang Junfeng
Nankai University Media Alumni

王烁皓
南开大学物理科学学院 2018 级本科生
Wang Shuohao
Undergraduate Student of Grade 2018, School of Physics of Nankai University

王晓明
天津电视台记者、《今晚报》原摄影记者
Wang Xiaoming
Journalist of Tianjin TV Station and former photographer of Tonight News Paper

王海琦
南开大学宣传部新闻中心摄像记者
Wang Haiqi
Camera Reporter of News Center of Publicity Department of Nankai University

韦承金
南开大学宣传部新闻中心编辑
Wei Chengjin
Editor of News Center of Publicity Department of Nankai University

田雨
南开大学艺术教育中心教师
Tian Yu
Teacher of Art Education Center of Nankai University

史嵩
《中老年时报》摄影记者
Shi Song
Middle-aged and Old Times Photographer

吕军
南开大学保卫处教师
Lyu Jun
Security Teacher of Nankai University

任永华
南开大学宣传部新闻中心记者
Ren Yonghua
Journalist of the News Center of the Publicity Department of Nankai University

任梦昕
南开大学物理科学学院教师
Ren Mengxin
Teacher of School of Physics of Nankai University

多吉次仁
热心人士
Dogi Tshiren
Enthusiasts

刘东岳
《天津教育报》摄影记者
Liu Dongyue
Photographer of Tianjin Education Daily

刘瑞麒
南开大学汉语言文化学院 2018 届硕士毕业生
Liu Ruiqi
2018 Graduates of Master's Degree, College of Chinese Language and Culture of Nankai University

李杰
南开大学药物化学生物学国家重点实验室博士后
Li Jie
Postdoctoral Program of the State Key Laboratory of Medicinal Chemical Biology, Nankai University

李晓彤
南开大学体育部教工
Li Xiaotong
Faculty of Sports Department of Nankai University

李想
《天津教育报》原摄影记者
Li Xiang
Former Photographer of Tianjin Education Daily

杨玉诚
南开大学商学院 2018 级本科生
Yang Yucheng
Grade 2018 Undergraduates of Nankai University Business School

吴军辉
南开大学宣传部新闻中心记者
Wu Junhui
Journalist of the News Center of the Publicity Department of Nankai University

沈岳
《天津工人报》摄影记者
Shen Yue
Photographer of Tianjin Workers Daily

张立

《今晚报》摄影记者

Zhang Li

Photographer of Tonight News Paper

张珀瑜

热心市民

Zhang Poyu

Enthusiastic citizen

张树楠

南开大学文学院教师

Zhang Shunan

School of Literature, Nankai University

张剑影

南开大学药学院教师

Zhang Jianying

College of Pharmacy, Nankai University

张哲浩

南开大学 2016 级周恩来政府管理学院本科生

Zhang Zhehao

Grade 2016 Undergraduate of Zhou Enlai School of Government, Nankai University

张道正

中国新闻社记者

Zhang Daozheng

Journalist of China News Agency

范波

热心人士

Fan Bo

Enthusiasts

林坤洋

南开大学周恩来政府管理学院 2017 级本科生

Lin Kunyang

Grade 2017 Undergraduate of Zhou Enlai School of Government, Nankai University

姜丙骏

南开大学周恩来政府管理学院 2017 级本科生

Jiang Bingjun

Grade 2017 Undergraduate of Zhou Enlai School of Government, Nankai University

姜宝成

《天津日报》摄影记者

Jiang Baocheng

Photographer of Tianjin Daily

聂际慈

南开大学宣传部新闻中心记者

Nie Jici

Journalist of the News Center of the Publicity Department of Nankai University

贾真珍

南开大学药物化学生物学国家重点实验室 2019 届博士毕业生

Jia Zhenzhen

Ph.D. Graduate of the State Key Laboratory of Medicinal Chemical Biology, Nankai University, 2019

高珊

南开大学药物化学生物学国家重点实验室 2017 级博士研究生

Gao Shan

Ph.D. Grade 2017, State Key Laboratory of Medicinal Chemical Biology, Nankai University

高鹏

"南以离开"摄影工作室创始人

Gao Peng

Founder of "Nan Yi Li Kai" Photo Studio ("Nan Yi Li Kai" has the same pronunciation as "hard to leave Nankai" in Chinese)

常小松

南开大学文学院 2018 届硕士毕业生

Chang Xiaosong

2018 Graduate of Master's Degree of Literature, Nankai University

游思行

腾讯网编辑、原《渤海早报》摄影记者

You Sihang

Editor of Tencent Net and Photographer of Bohai Morning Post

（按姓氏笔画排序）

（Ranking by surname strokes）

后记

　　这本图集酝酿于 2018 年底，恰逢南开大学即将迎来建校 100 周年的历史时刻。党委宣传部新闻中心作为学校新闻宣传的信息中枢，肩负着外树形象、内聚人心的重要使命，同时于日常工作中也记录下了南开大学这座巍巍学府的点点滴滴。在文字记者的笔尖下、在摄影记者的镜头里，一个个鲜活的南开人、一件件生动的南开事、一处处美丽的南开景，汇聚起了南开大学爱国报国的百年探索，树立起了南开人立公增能、秉公尽能的精神品格。奋斗的姿态最美丽，百年南开正青春，我们意在用图片勾勒出那些与青春、与南开、与奋斗有关的图景，以此献礼南开大学百年华诞。

　　感谢学校和宣传部领导。你们关心、关注着每一位奋战在新闻宣传一线的记者们，鼓励他们通过新闻报道把南开人的担当意识、公能品格、奉献精神传递到更广阔的天地，并为他们的未来发展创造广阔舞台，特别是在本图集的策划、约稿、联系出版等方面，提供着帮助与支持、鼓励与认可。

　　感谢本书所有作者。你们当中有南开大学各部门的同事，有南开教师，有爱好摄影的同学，有在显微镜下发现"新世界"的科研人员，有长期与南开保持良好合作关系的媒体记者，有关心母校发展的热心校友，有在各个场合感动于南开精神的普通市民，也有生活在南开园的摄影创业者。本图集中大部分图片为近 10 年作品。一张好照片的背后，是一个有爱的灵魂，是一颗炽热的红心，是一段与南开有关的故事，是一份浓厚的南开情结。如今，感谢你们以志愿者的身份提供了这些珍贵的照片，与读者一同分享你们眼中的南开，分享这方富有青春气息的美丽校园。

　　感谢所有帮助我们的人。你们中有文学院编辑出版学专业的学生、有英语培训机构的创业校友、有南开大学官方微信的学生团队、有擅长航拍的学生团队，完成这本书的编校需要克服一定的困难，无论是整体策划还是文案撰写、装帧设计等等，都花费了大量的心血，但我们乐在其中。

　　在编辑过程中，我们从 500G、5 万余张投稿作品中甄选出入册的 233 幅图片，尽量全面真实地保留了它们的原样，意图传递给读者趣味与美的享受，但由于水平、时间所限，编校中可能仍有错漏之处，望广大读者不吝批评，提出宝贵意见。

　　祝愿南开大学永远年青！

Postscript

The idea of this photo album came into shape at the end of 2018, when we were approaching the historic moment of the Centennial of Nankai University. As the information hub of the university's news and publicity, the News Center of the Party Committee Publicity Department shoulders the important task of building a proper image externally and uniting minds and hearts internally while it also records the dribs and drabs of this magnificent university. At the pen tip of a text reporter and in the lens of a photo journalist, every lively Nankai person, every vivid Nankai event and every beautiful Nankai scene together have formed the one hundred years of Nankai's exploration of patriotism, and have created Nankai's spirit of dedication and service to public interest with all-round capability. An enterprising soul is the most beautiful. Nankai at the age of 100 is still in its youth. We want to greet the Centennial of Nankai University with these photos telling stories of youth, of Nankai and of diligence.

Our gratitude goes to the leaders of the University and the Publicity Department. You care about and pay attention to every journalist working at the news and publicity frontline, encourage them to pass on the sense of ownership, the character of serving and the spirit of dedication of Nankai people to the wider world through their news reports, and create a broad stage for their future development. You have especially provided assistance, support, encouragement and recognition to the planning, drafting, and publishing of this photo album.

Our gratitude goes to all the authors of this photo album. Among you are colleagues from various departments of Nankai University, teachers from Nankai, students who are interested in photography, researchers who have discovered the "New World" under the microscope, media reporters who have long-time and good cooperation with Nankai, enthusiastic alumni who are concerned for the development of Nankai, ordinary citizens who are moved by the Nankai spirit on various occasions, and photographers who live on campus. Most of the photos in this album were taken in the past ten years. Behind each photo is a loving soul, a fervent heart, a story related to Nankai, and a strong connection with Nankai. Now, we'd like to thank you for volunteering to provide these precious photos to share with our readers the Nankai University in your eyes and this beautiful and youthful campus.

Our gratitude goes to all who have helped us. Among you are students majoring in editing and publishing in the School of Literature, alumni who set up English training schools, student teams from official We Chat of Nankai University and a team of students who excel at aerial photography. Editing and proofreading this album required us to overcome difficulties in all aspects, including overall planning, copywriting, binding design and others. It took a lot of efforts, but we enjoyed it.

In the process of editing, we have selected 233 photos from a 500 GB pool of more than 50,000 photos we received. We tried our best to keep the selected photos as they are to present their original taste and beauty to the readers. But due to capability and time limits, there might still be mistakes and omissions, and we welcome corrections and valuable opinions from our readers.

May Nankai University be young forever!

南开大学建校100周年

NANKAI UNIVERSITY

100th Anniversary